Faith, Hope & Love

THIS PLANNER BELONGS TO:

_____

SIMPLY
SOULFUL DESIGNS
™

Author of prayers - *Rev. Whitney Wilkinson Arreche*

Co-author & illustrator -

BECKY BAKER

ARTIST

Welcome! I offer these prayers to guide you deeper into communion with God, yourself, and your neighbor. Some of these prayers are communal in nature, and others are deeply personal. Some of these prayers are designed to bring comfort, and others are designed to stir us from complacency. Know that as you pray these prayers, I pray for you, that each day of this year will bring new life, new hope, new vision, and new action. May God be with you all.

*~ **Rev. Whitney Wilkinson Arreche***

About the Authors

Rev. Whitney Wilkinson Arreche

Bio

Rev. Whitney Wilkinson Arreche (she/her/hers) is a Presbyterian Church (U.S.A.) minister of word and sacrament, and a Doctor of Theology (ThD) candidate at Duke University set to graduate December 2022. She researches the ways language creates particular power relationships, particularly the language of racial reconciliation in Christianity, popular culture, and politics. She has served churches in Belfast, Northern Ireland and in rural North Carolina. She serves as the chairperson of the Presbyterian Church (U.S.A.) General Assembly Committee for Ecumenical and Interreligious Relations. She represents her denomination on the National Council of Churches Matters of Faith and Theological Order (Faith and Order) Convening Table. She has presented her research nationally and internationally at religion, theology, and social theory conferences. She has been published in the Christian Century, the Presbyterian Outlook, Presbyterians Today, and Political Theology Network. She is a contributing author to an upcoming theological volume, the T&T Clark Theological Encyclopedia (Bloomsbury). Most recently, she contributed to the book Liberating Church: A 21st Century Hush Harbor Manifesto (Voices, Wipf and Stock, 2022), drawing wisdom and power from the antebellum hush harbors to proclaim a Christianity unbeholden to White supremacy. She is a scholar, a writer, and a teacher, but mostly, she is a pastor. She lives in Texas with her spouse Carlos and their dog, Fifi.

Her website is https://whitneywilkinsonarreche.com

Becky Baker

Bio

Becky Baker is a self taught artist as well as a mom, grandmother, dog mom and creator of Simply Soulful Designs ™. She was an entrepreneur in her own small business for 29 years to which she retired from in 2020. She's now taking the time to enjoy life to the fullest, working part time and by fulfilling her creative passions!

Dear reader,

First and foremost, I cannot express my gratitude enough to Rev. Whitney Wilkinson Arreche for her contribution to this book. It is a treasure I will hold near and dear in my heart, always.

My personal goal is to have the intention to be mindful in what I create and in everything I say and do every day. Yet knowing and realizing that there is no such thing as absolute perfection. My hope is that this comes through to you in this body of work.

I invite you to show up for yourself this year in this planner. Plan some fun into your weeks! Allow your activities to be filled with wonder and curiousity. Go out and truly experience what this magnificant gorgeous planet we live on has to offer. To put it quite simply, permit yourself to embody the true spirit of being fully alive! Immerse yourself in these prayers and allow Grace to walk with you! I know, I will read them over and over. I placed a few coloring pages in this book for your enjoyment. So please, color them in! Don't be fussy about creating a masterpiece with any of it. Give yourself permission to be imperfect. Allow your inner child artist to come out to play and feel the joy in making this book, and this year, all yours!

To me, showing up for ourselves is as important as it is to show up for others. Also, focusing on our awareness to be present in all situations and to try do the best we can. Life here on earth can be so stressful and difficult to navigate. At some point, for all of us, it becomes complicated with suffering. I believe we all need inspiration and kindness to show up, especially in those difficult times. I also believe that no matter who we are, or where we are in our journey, we can decide at any point to simplify and enhance our lives by choosing to walk a much slower, more thoughtful and soulful path.

It is my heartfelt wish for you that your year be filled with joyful events to treasure. If hardship happens to cross your doorstep, may you find comfort and peace in your faith. May all those you know, or those who are with you at this time, surround you with kindness. And may you have the ability to forgive those that do not.

Peace be with you,

~ Becky

YEAR AT A GLANCE

JANUARY 2023

S	M	T	W	T	F	S
1	2	3	4	5	6	7
8	9	10	11	12	13	14
15	16	17	18	19	20	21
22	23	24	25	26	27	28
29	30	31	1	2	3	4

FEBRUARY 2023

S	M	T	W	T	F	S
29	30	31	1	2	3	4
5	6	7	8	9	10	11
12	13	14	15	16	17	18
19	20	21	22	23	24	25

MARCH 2023

S	M	T	W	T	F	S
26	27	28	1	2	3	4
5	6	7	8	9	10	11
12	13	14	15	16	17	18
19	20	21	22	23	24	25

APRIL 2023

S	M	T	W	T	F	S
26	27	28	29	30	31	1
2	3	4	5	6	7	8
9	10	11	12	13	14	15
16	17	18	19	20	21	22
23	24	25	26	27	28	29

MAY 2023

S	M	T	W	T	F	S
30	1	2	3	4	5	6
7	8	9	10	11	12	13
14	15	16	17	18	19	20
21	22	23	24	25	26	27
28	29	30	31	1	2	3

JUNE 2023

S	M	T	W	T	F	S
28	29	30	31	1	2	3
4	5	6	7	8	9	10
11	12	13	14	15	16	17
18	19	20	21	22	23	24
25	26	27	28	29	30	1

notes

JULY 2023

S	M	T	W	T	F	S
25	26	27	28	29	30	1
2	3	4	5	6	7	8
9	10	11	12	13	14	15
16	17	18	19	20	21	22
23	24					

AUGUST 2023

S	M	T	W	T	F	S
30	31	1	2	3	4	5
6	7	8	9	10	11	12
13	14	15	16	17	18	19
20	21	22	23	24	25	26

SEPTEMBER 2023

S	M	T	W	T	F	S
27	28	29	30	31	1	2
3	4	5	6	7	8	9
10	11	12	13	14	15	16
17	18	19	20	21	22	23

OCTOBER 2023

S	M	T	W	T	F	S
1	2	3	4	5	6	7
8	9	10	11	12	13	14
15	16	17	18	19	20	21
22	23	24	25	26	27	28
29	30	31	1	2	3	4

NOVEMBER 2023

S	M	T	W	T	F	S
29	30	31	1	2	3	4
5	6	7	8	9	10	11
12	13	14	15	16	17	18
19	20	21	22	23	24	25
26	27	28	29	30	1	2

DECEMBER 2023

S	M	T	W	T	F	S
26	27	28	29	30	1	2
3	4	5	6	7	8	9
10	11	12	13	14	15	16
17	18	19	20	21	22	23
24						

notes

JANUARY 2023

sunday	monday	tuesday	wednesday
Jan 1 New Year's Day	2	3	4
8	9	10	11
15	16 Martin Luther King Day	17	18
22	23	24	25
29	30	31	Feb 1

thursday	friday	saturday	notes
5	6	7	
12	13	14	
19	20	21	
26	27	28	
2	3	4	

A Breath Prayer

As you begin this day,
Take a moment to breathe,
and feel centered in your body and spirit.

Close your eyes.

Take a deep breath in, and out.
Breathe in the goodness of the holy one.
Breathe it out to others.

Relax your shoulders and neck.
Feel what is yours to carry.
Feel what God carries for you.

Soften the tension in your jaw.
May God be with you in your speaking,
and in your listening.

Ease the tightness around your eyes.
May the divine give you the vision you need
for this moment, for this time.

Open your hands gently.
May you receive understanding and wisdom
from others. May we hold each other with care.

Open your eyes.
May you see yourself as you are, and as you can be.
May you see others as our creator does.

Again, take a deep breath in, and out.
Breathe in the goodness of the holy one.
Breathe it out to others.
Amen.

JANUARY 2023

29 thursday

30 friday

31 saturday

1 sunday

New Year's Eve

New Year's Day

JANUARY 2023

2 monday

3 tuesday

4 wednesday

5 thursday

6 friday

7 saturday

8 sunday

JANUARY 2023

9 monday

10 tuesday

11 wednesday

12 thursday

13 friday

14 saturday

15 sunday

JANUARY 2023

16 monday

Martin Luther King Day

17 tuesday

18 wednesday

19 thursday

20 friday

21 saturday

22 sunday

JANUARY 2023

23 monday

24 tuesday

25 wednesday

26 thursday

27 friday

28 saturday

29 sunday

JANUARY 2023

30 monday

31 tuesday

1 wednesday

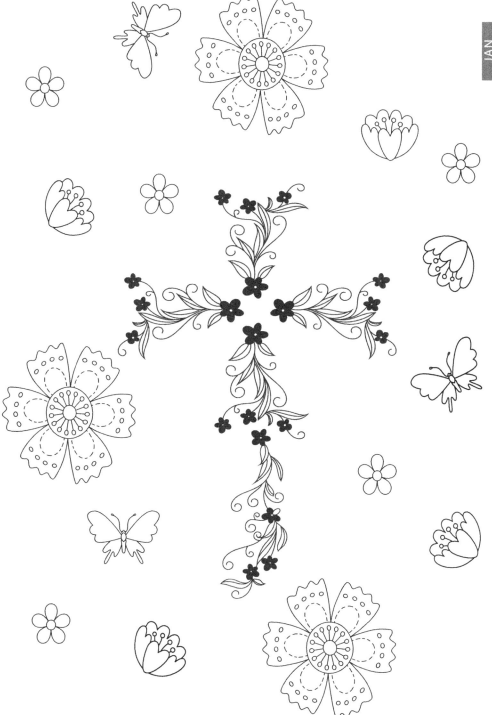

FEBRUARY 2023

sunday	monday	tuesday	wednesday
29	30	31	Feb 1
5	6	7	8
12	13	14 Valentine's Day	15
19	20 Presidents' Day	21	22
26	27	28	Mar 1

thursday	friday	saturday	notes
2	3	4	
9	10	11	
16	17	18	
23	24	25	
2	3	4	

A Prayer for Emptying

What does it mean that you are sovereign, God?
Does it mean you direct our days with a heavy,
strong hand? Marshalling us into obedience and servitude?
Does it mean that creation is for the exercise of your
dominion, for you to show your power and might?
Or maybe, does your sovereignty mean something
more like a pouring out: an emptying of the political words that
do nothing. An emptying of religion that only serves to make
a show of itself, to gain votes and money and power.
An emptying of the very heavens themselves,
raining down upon a weary world with something
like joy.

An emptying of our theologies of safety and comfort that we
may be filled with the courage and creativity of the
wild dreamers and builders of new worlds.
An emptying of our borders of church walls and
building projects and bottom lines, so that we can
remember what it really means to be your people,
to do church and not incorporate it,
to live who we say you are in our every moment.
An emptying of our deep places of despair and fear
and rage and insecurity, so that we can be filled like
cracked cups overflowing still with a grace that cannot
be contained.
If this is what it means for you to be our sovereign God, we
welcome it.
We welcome you, birther of new worlds and new life,
to come and disrupt our patterns that serve neither us
nor you
nor our neighbor.
We welcome you, birther of new worlds and new life,
to create something alive in us,
even now,
especially now.
Amen.

FEBRUARY 2023

30 monday

31 tuesday

1 wednesday

2 thursday

3 friday

4 saturday

5 sunday

FEBRUARY 2023

6 monday

7 tuesday

8 wednesday

9 thursday

10 friday

11 saturday

12 sunday

FEBRUARY 2023

13 monday

14 tuesday

Valentine's Day

15 wednesday

16 thursday

17 friday

18 saturday

19 sunday

FEBRUARY 2023

20 monday

Presidents' Day

21 tuesday

22 wednesday

23 thursday

24 friday

25 saturday

26 sunday

FEBRUARY 2023

27 monday

28 tuesday

1 wednesday

MARCH 2023

sunday	monday	tuesday	wednesday
26	27	28	Mar 1
5	6	7	8
12	13	14	15
19	20	21	22
26	27	28	29

thursday	friday	saturday	notes
2	3	4	
9	10	11	
16	17 St. Patrick's Day	18	
23	24	25	
30	31	Apr 1	

Prayers of the People

God of compassion and courage,
Hear our prayers for the grieving:
        Those who have lost loved ones to disease
        Those who have lost loved ones to hatred
        Those who have lost loved ones to indifference and injustice.
        Bring comfort, solace, and even, joy.

Hear our prayers for the struggling:
        Those who face addiction
        Those who face financial hardship
        Those who face painful relationships and loss of purpose.
        Bring the equitable distribution of wealth, and a path forward.

Hear our prayers for the comfortable:
        Those who think they've earned what they have
        Those who need to make a name for themselves
        Those who believe they are perfect.
        Bring humility, generosity, and honesty.

Hear our prayers for your church:
        Those churches who are dwindling
        Those churches who are thriving
        Those many who are somewhere in between.
        Your clergy who are weathered, worn, exhausted.
        Bring vision beyond a building, and bring a
        true concern for others, and sabbath rest.

Hear our prayers for ourselves:
        Those who feel enlivened by you
        Those who feel very little
        Those who feel dread, or anxiety, or worry.
        Those who feel hope, or peace, or love.
        Bring a sharing of burdens and a sharing of joys.
        Bring a real relationship between us. Amen.

MARCH 2023

27 monday

28 tuesday

1 wednesday

2 thursday

3 friday

4 saturday

5 sunday

MARCH 2023

6 monday

7 tuesday

8 wednesday

9 thursday

10 friday

11 saturday

12 sunday

MARCH 2023

13 monday

14 tuesday

15 wednesday

16 thursday

17 friday

St. Patrick's Day

18 saturday

19 sunday

MARCH 2023

20 monday

21 tuesday

22 wednesday

23 thursday

24 friday

25 saturday

26 sunday

MARCH 2023

27 monday

28 tuesday

29 wednesday

30 thursday

31 friday

1 saturday   2 sunday

APRIL 2023

sunday	monday	tuesday	wednesday
26	27	28	29
2	3	4	5
9 Easter	10	11	12
16	17	18	19
23 / 30	24	25	26

thursday	friday	saturday	notes
30	31	Apr 1	
6	7	8	
13	14	15	
20	21	22	
27	28	29	

APR

A Prayer for Stillness

This day, God, just for this day, I commit to become
stiller, quieter, and open.
I will stop, if only for a moment, the need to do
more, earn more, prove more.
I will quiet my overworked heart and
give my frenetic brain a break.
I will simply be.
I will not feel guilty for naps on the couch with the dog,
or for long lingerings over hot coffee,
"cogitating", as my grandmother would say.
I will not endlessly scroll my life away on a phone,
and I will not listen to the voice telling me I
have to prove my worth.
I will, this day, simply be.
I will listen to my body and honor what she needs.
I will rest when I need rest, eat when I need food,
drink when I need water, and move when I need to move.
This day I will feel, deep in these tired bones,
That I am enough.
That you are enough.
That this day is enough.

APRIL 2023

30 thursday

31 friday

1 saturday

2 sunday

APRIL 2023

3 monday

4 tuesday

5 wednesday

6 thursday

7 friday

8 saturday

9 sunday

Easter

APRIL 2023

10 monday

11 tuesday

12 wednesday

13 thursday

14 friday

15 saturday

16 sunday

APRIL 2023

17 monday

_____

18 tuesday

_____

19 wednesday

_____

20 thursday

21 friday

22 saturday

23 sunday

APRIL 2023

24 monday

_____
_____
_____
_____
_____

25 tuesday

_____
_____
_____
_____
_____

26 wednesday

_____
_____
_____
_____

27 thursday

28 friday

29 saturday

30 sunday

MAY 2023

sunday	monday	tuesday	wednesday
30	May 1	2	3
7	8	9	10
14 Mother's Day	15	16	17
21	22	23	24
28	29 Memorial Day	30	31

thursday	friday	saturday	notes
4	5	6	
11	12	13	
18	19	20	
25	26	27	
Jun 1	2	3	

MAY

A Prayer for Wisdom

God, who weaves the world together in wisdom:
give us even the tiniest taste of your wisdom.
Our lives are flooded with words:
With news stories of bigotry, hatred, violence, and suffering.
With tweets and posts that dice our days into tiny
bites that turn to sawdust in our mouths,
leaving us ravenous.
With the emotional whiplash of
announcements, policies, and press conferences
reigniting the anxiety, and the anger.

So many words swirl around us, and overwhelm us.
And we do what feels safest to us,
which is to form action plans and mission statements,
as if our words will make this flood of our time obey us.
As if our words will calm the flood waters of
grief within us.
Underneath all of these words, these
efforts of ordering
what can't be ordered
and explaining
what can't be explained
of performing our lives for
the consumption of others
rather than living them
there is a common word:
fear.

We are afraid of our own mortality.
We are afraid we are meaningless.
We are afraid we will revert into
our smaller, sadder selves of six or twelve months ago.

And so when we ask for your wisdom to come
amidst all this noise
and all this fear
we must also ask that you come in a way
we do not expect.
In a way we cannot
plan, organize, schedule, or commodify.
You will have to surprise us.
You who came not as a mighty monarch to establish your
reign over all lesser people,
but as a curious child.

You will have to weave your wisdom into the
spaces between all the
words, the chaos of our days.
And maybe – if you are as good as you say you are,
if you are as good as we say you are –
you will even bring your wisdom through
joy.
Joy that sends the fear away
empty
and fills up every crack
of these fractured lives of ours
to the brim
and overflows with a deep
knowledge – a wisdom –
of your goodness towards us, and our capacity
to be good to each other.

May it be so.

MAY 2023

1 monday

2 tuesday

3 wednesday

4 thursday

5 friday

6 saturday

7 sunday

MAY 2023

8 monday

9 tuesday

10 wednesday

11 thursday

12 friday

13 saturday

14 sunday

Mother's Day

MAY 2023

15 monday

16 tuesday

17 wednesday

18 thursday

19 friday

20 saturday

21 sunday

MAY 2023

22 monday

23 tuesday

24 wednesday

25 thursday

26 friday

27 saturday

28 sunday

MAY 2023

29 monday

Memorial Day

30 tuesday

31 wednesday

JUNE 2023

sunday	monday	tuesday	wednesday
28	29 Memorial Day	30	31
4	5	6	7
11	12	13	14
18 Father's Day	19	20	21
25	26	27	28

thursday	friday	saturday	notes
Jun 1	2	3	
8	9	10	
15	16	17	
22	23	24	
29	30	Jul 1	

A Prayer for Ancestors

I thank you, God, for the faith of my ancestors.
I thank you for those who trusted you through hardships I will never
understand.
I thank you for those whose love made my life possible.
I thank you for their courage, and their compassion.
I pray that I will honor them with my life.
And I thank you for the gift of change.
Help me to honor the best of who they were
while also
being the best of who I can be today.
Help me break patterns of intergenerational pain
and harm.
Help me practice the sort of justice they may not have
even dreamed of.
Help me honor their legacy by being kind, loving,
truthful, and good.
And be with those who will come after me,
guiding them into a future I myself
cannot yet imagine. A future that I pray is
kinder, more loving, and more honest
than the world I live in.
Thank you for those who come before, and
thank for those who come after.
Thank you that we are part of a legacy even as
we can do new beautiful things with that legacy.
God of our yesterdays and our todays and our tomorrows,

be with us all. Amen.

JUNE 2023

1 thursday

2 friday

3 saturday

4 sunday

JUNE 2023

5 monday

6 tuesday

7 wednesday

8 thursday

9 friday

10 saturday

11 sunday

JUNE 2023

12 monday

13 tuesday

14 wednesday

15 thursday

16 friday

17 saturday

18 sunday

Father's Day

JUNE 2023

19 monday

20 tuesday

21 wednesday

22 thursday

23 friday

24 saturday

25 sunday

JUNE 2023

26 monday

27 tuesday

28 wednesday

29 thursday

30 friday

1 saturday

2 sunday

JULY 2023

sunday	monday	tuesday	wednesday
25	26	27	28
2	3	4 Independence Day	5
9	10	11	12
16	17	18	19
23 30	24 31	25	26

thursday	friday	saturday	notes
29	30	Jul 1	
6	7	8	
13	14	15	
20	21	22	
27	28	29	

A Prayer for Anxiety

God, do you ever feel anxious?
Do you ever look at this world, with all of our stress
and war and worry and need
and find your heart unable to settle,
your eyes unable to close,
your mind unable to stop?
Maybe you, as the Breath that blows through
the world in love, Spirit, do not have moments
of panic, of shortened breath and shortened tempers.
Maybe you always have enough calm, enough breath.
But I do know this to be true: you see us.
You see me.
You never look away when I am feeling overwhelmed with the
world and my life.
You come, Spirit of life, calming each breath, reminding me that
I am safe
I am okay
I am not alone.
And you come, sometimes slowly,
filling the pit of a stomach heavy with worry
with something like joy.
You wait out the storm of worry, sleeping by
our sides,
reassuring us,
reassuring me,
until the storm breaks,
and the sun shines through the clouds.
You sit with us when we are not okay.
(and you never make us feel guilt for feeling not okay)
You are so good to us.
And with a God as good as you,
ever beside us,
ever caring,
we can find our breath,
and calm our hearts,
and quiet our minds.
Thank you.

JULY 2023

29 thursday

30 friday

1 saturday

2 sunday

JULY 2023

3 monday

4 tuesday

Independence Day

5 wednesday

6 thursday

7 friday

8 saturday

9 sunday

JULY 2023

10 monday

11 tuesday

12 wednesday

13 thursday

14 friday

15 saturday

16 sunday

JULY 2023

17 monday

18 tuesday

19 wednesday

20 thursday

21 friday

22 saturday

23 sunday

JULY 2023

24 monday

25 tuesday

26 wednesday

27 thursday

28 friday

29 saturday

30 sunday

JULY 2023

31 monday

1 tuesday

2 wednesday

AUGUST 2023

sunday	monday	tuesday	wednesday
30	31	Aug 1	2
6	7	8	9
13	14	15	16
20	21	22	23
27	28	29	30

thursday	friday	saturday	notes
3	4	5	
10	11	12	
17	18	19	
24	25	26	
31	Sep 1	2	

A Prayer for Abundance

Abundant God, sometimes we imagine you in such a
small way.
We have believed that you care more about control than anything else.
And so we put you in a box, too small to contain even
a fraction of you.
And we defend you from what we perceive to be threats,
which are really only threats to our ideas.
We box you in with words and ideas
and borders and truths,
and before we even realize it,
we have trapped ourselves as well.
And yet, you who broke out of a tomb,
you who broke norms of your day,
refuse to be boxed in.
You show us that you are so much bigger than we
have believed.
You show us that our lives can be so much bigger than we
have lived.
And you invite us to consider a life not of
self-denial and judgment and fear and comfortable prejudice,
but a life of radical abundance.
Where we proclaim that you want us to live this
fleeting life
fully alive
fully present
fully immersed in all the experiences and wonders
you have for us.
What energy we find for joy when we stop boxing you
and ourselves and others in!
What acceptance and abundance we encounter.
Break open the boxes.
Unbind us and let us go. Amen.

Every sunset is an opportunity to reset. Every sunrise begins with new eyes

AUGUST 2023

31 monday

1 tuesday

2 wednesday

3 thursday

4 friday

5 saturday

6 sunday

AUGUST 2023

7 monday

8 tuesday

9 wednesday

10 thursday

11 friday

12 saturday

13 sunday

AUGUST 2023

14 monday

15 tuesday

16 wednesday

17 thursday

18 friday

19 saturday

20 sunday

AUGUST 2023

21 monday

22 tuesday

23 wednesday

24 thursday

25 friday

26 saturday

27 sunday

AUGUST 2023

28 monday

29 tuesday

30 wednesday

31 thursday

1 friday

2 saturday

3 sunday

SEPTEMBER 2023

sunday	monday	tuesday	wednesday
27	28	29	30
3	4 Labor Day	5	6
10	11	12	13
17	18	19	20
24	25	26	27

thursday	friday	saturday	notes
31	Sep 1	2	
7	8	9	
14	15	16	
21	22	23	
28	29	30	

SEP

A Prayer for Listening

Today, God, is a day for listening.
I will listen for your voice in the wind in the trees.
I will listen for your voice in the singing of birds.
I will listen for your voice in the mischief of squirrels.
I will listen for your voice in the laughter of children.
I will listen for your voice in the beating of my own heart.
I will listen for your voice in the softness of a blanket.
I will listen for your voice in the eyes of a stranger.
I will listen for your voice in the smell of comforting food.
I will listen for your voice in the busyness of work.
I will listen for your voice in the spaces filled with silence.
I will listen for your voice in the steadfast shining of stars.
I will listen for your voice in the moments waiting for sleep to come.
I will listen to your voice today.
I will listen.
Will you speak?

Gratitude makes sense of our past, brings peace for today, and creates a vision for tomorrow

be still

PSALM 46:10

SEPTEMBER 2023

31 thursday

1 friday

2 saturday

3 sunday

SEP

SEPTEMBER 2023

4 monday

Labor Day

5 tuesday

6 wednesday

7 thursday

8 friday

9 saturday

10 sunday

SEPTEMBER 2023

11 monday

12 tuesday

13 wednesday

14 thursday

15 friday

16 saturday

17 sunday

SEPTEMBER 2023

18 monday

19 tuesday

20 wednesday

21 thursday

22 friday

23 saturday

24 sunday

SEPTEMBER 2023

25 monday

26 tuesday

27 wednesday

28 thursday

29 friday

30 saturday

1 sunday

OCTOBER 2023

sunday	monday	tuesday	wednesday
Oct 1	2	3	4
8	9 Columbus Day	10	11
15	16	17	18
22	23	24	25
29	30	31 Halloween	Nov 1

thursday	friday	saturday	notes
5	6	7	
12	13	14	
19	20	21	
26	27	28	
2	3	4	

OCT

A Prayer for Action

What are we waiting for?
So much of our lives are spent waiting, God.
We wait to act until we know all possible
outcomes, expecting the worst.
We wait to love until we know the recipient will
give it back, making it transactional.
We wait for things to get better,
for our bodies to be stronger,
for our minds to be clearer,
for our hearts to feel comfortable.
And waiting becomes doing nothing.
Because maybe we never are fully ready
to love
to act
to trust.
Maybe we never feel completely prepared.
Maybe you, God, did not feel completely prepared
for all you encountered on this earth.
And yet still, you walked,
even on water.
You loved,
especially those no one else did.
You healed,
even when it put your own body on the line.
You acted,
again and again, not because you were ready,
but because it needed to be done.
So help us stop waiting,
and start becoming the people
we need;
the people this world
needs.
Just because we cannot do all things
does not mean
we cannot do
some things.
Let's begin.

OCTOBER 2023

28 thursday

29 friday

30 saturday

1 sunday

OCT

OCTOBER 2023

2 monday

3 tuesday

4 wednesday

5 thursday

6 friday

7 saturday

8 sunday

OCTOBER 2023

9 monday

Columbus Day

10 tuesday

11 wednesday

12 thursday

13 friday

14 saturday

15 sunday

OCT

OCTOBER 2023

16 monday

17 tuesday

18 wednesday

19 thursday

20 friday

21 saturday

22 sunday

OCTOBER 2023

23 monday

24 tuesday

25 wednesday

26 thursday

27 friday

28 saturday

29 sunday

OCT

OCTOBER 2023

30 monday

31 tuesday

Halloween

1 wednesday

NOVEMBER 2023

sunday	monday	tuesday	wednesday
29	30	31 Halloween	Nov 1
5	6	7	8
12	13	14	15
19	20	21	22
26	27	28	29

thursday	friday	saturday	notes
2	3	4	
9	10	11 Veterans Day	
16	17	18	
23 Thanksgiving	24	25	
30	Dec 1	2	

NOV

A Blessing of Difference

God, we thank you for the gift of difference.
Too often, difference is a thing to be feared,
or managed,
or ordered,
or theologized.
And yet, with you, difference is beautiful,
adding richness to life
and variety to this world.
The fact that we are not all the same
is proof of your unwavering
creativity
artistry
vision and
love.
Forgive us when we make difference a threat,
or make our own particularities idols to worship.
Forgive us when we let our fear of difference become
violent.
Move us, especially those of us with the
most power and influence,
to a place where difference is to be celebrated.
Where we do not build our identities by tearing down
the bodies of others.
Also move us to a place where we do not ignore
difference,
assuming a universality that
never was.
But rather, give us the vision to appreciate difference
rightly,
neither valorizing it nor
ignoring it.
So that we might find a belonging that does not require
anyone to be less, and that does not require
anyone to be more.
A belonging where difference is beautiful,
a sign of your creativity
artistry
vision and
love.
Amen.

NOVEMBER 2023

30 monday

31 tuesday

Halloween

1 wednesday

2 thursday

3 friday

4 saturday

5 sunday

NOVEMBER 2023

6 monday

7 tuesday

8 wednesday

9 thursday

10 friday

11 saturday

12 sunday

NOV

Veterans Day

NOVEMBER 2023

13 monday

14 tuesday

15 wednesday

16 thursday

17 friday

18 saturday

19 sunday

NOVEMBER 2023

20 monday

21 tuesday

22 wednesday

23 thursday

Thanksgiving

24 friday

25 saturday

26 sunday

NOVEMBER 2023

27 monday

28 tuesday

29 wednesday

30 thursday

1 friday

2 saturday

3 sunday

NOV

DECEMBER 2023

sunday	monday	tuesday	wednesday
26	27	28	29
3	4	5	6
10	11	12	13
17	18	19	20
24 New Year's Day 31	25 Christmas Day	26	27

thursday	friday	saturday	notes
30	Dec 1	2	
7	8	9	
14	15	16	
21	22	23	
28	29	30	

DEC

A Prayer for Worth

Creator of the cosmos,
we can now see the heavens better than ever before.
Swirling galaxies,
dusty star trails,
gas giants, and
nebulas,
and supernovas,
and planets.
It can make us feel very small.
And we are.
Our lives are but fleeting dust in the story
of the heavens.
And yet, you give each of us the potential
to shine.
We are all made in your image –
the image of love –
and can bring goodness and even
wonder
to this world.
Help us look to the heavens not to feel our own
insignificance,
but to feel our
worth.
Help us not waste a single second of this life on
shrinking or hedging or being less than
the unique creatures you have made us to be.
Help us to see our lives as intermingled with
the lives of galaxies,
showing the beautiful and heartbreaking cycles of
life and death.
The stars do not apologize for shining.
The supernovas do not try to take up less space.
The galaxies do not shy away from their interdependence.
Our lives are but a speck in the cosmos, but we can do so much
with our time.
We can love.
We can give.
We can live.
We can shine.

Always
be
joyful

DECEMBER 2023

1 friday

2 saturday

3 sunday

DEC

DECEMBER 2023

4 monday

5 tuesday

6 wednesday

7 thursday

8 friday

9 saturday

10 sunday

DEC

DECEMBER 2023

11 monday

12 tuesday

13 wednesday

14 thursday

15 friday

16 saturday

17 sunday

DECEMBER 2023

18 monday

19 tuesday

20 wednesday

21 thursday

22 friday

23 saturday

24 sunday

DECEMBER 2023

25 monday

Christmas Day

26 tuesday

27 wednesday

28 thursday

29 friday

30 saturday

31 sunday

New Year's Eve

DEC

JANUARY 2024

sunday	monday	tuesday	wednesday
31	Jan 1 New Year's Day	2	3
7	8	9	10
14	15	16	17
21	22	23	24
28	29	30	31

thursday	friday	saturday	notes
4	5	6	
11	12	13	
18	19	20	
25	26	27	
Feb 1	2	3	

NOTES

NOTES

NOTES

Made in the USA
Middletown, DE
23 December 2022

20325245R00106